GOLDFISH

KEEPING AND BREEDING
THEM IN CAPTIVITY

PHOTO BY FRED ROSENZWEIG.

A champion-quality Bubble-Eye goldfish.

By
Spencer Glass

CONTENTS

INTRODUCTION

I'll never forget that day I went into a local store and found myself enchanted by three kiddie pools filled to the brim with thousands of glittering, eye-catching Comet goldfish. You got a pair for free with every purchase! Well, of course this offer was more than my eight-year-old body could stand. I flew out of the store, hopped on my bike, banana seat and all, and headed home to inform my mother of this wonderful offer.

Naturally my mother was a little more cynical than I, but with some persistent whining and clever cajoling I was able to talk her into buying that yarn she *so desperately* needed; and with this purchase of a skein or two came the nifty acquisition of my first two little finned friends.

Wow! The store was even nice enough to give us a little container of food, too. We were set.

On the way home they were dubbed Junior & Dynamite. I was so thrilled. I could tell just by looking at them that they were as happy with me as I was with them. This was especially prevalent as we immediately

Comet goldfish are universally the most popular goldfish. They are by far the least expensive and are used as a home decoration as well as for live food for predatory pets such as larger fishes and snakes.

dumped them into one of my mother's brass colored gelatin molds. We simply added a little more tap water and presto! They were now part of my household.

I'm sure we all have stories like this about which we reflect upon. For many of us, our very first experience with fish at all was with a goldfish. Who can resist them either? They look right at you with those puppy-dog eyes, wag their tails, and seem to almost bark out the commands, "Feed me, love me, feed me!" And we do.

One thing is for sure, once you get started you're easily hooked (pardon the pun). Whether you obtained your first goldfish from the school carnival, from the jaws of another hungry fish, or from the kid next door, you'll find that these hardy characters offer more than just a fleeting fancy, kept up in a fish bowl. Having obtained your *first* goldfish, you are destined to make your way over to the neighborhood pet shop for food and various supplies. As you find yourself strolling down the various aisles of fish available, you are going to find that there is more to the goldfish family than just the *"plain old"* goldfish you have. You may even be aghast to find that many of your goldfish's cousins are known in the hobby as "feeder fish." Yes, these poor souls all too often find themselves as dinner fare for their larger brethren in the tropical fish family.

You'll soon see goldfish in more

You don't need a fancy dug-into-the-ground goldfish pond. You can enjoy your goldfish in a wading pool designed for small children. Of course if the above the ground pond can freeze solidly in the winter, the fish will have to be removed.

This very fancy goldfish is called *edonoshiki* in Japanese. It is called a *Calico Ranchu* in English. This fish is a male.

of a variety of shapes, sizes, and colors than you ever realized. Goldfish aren't just gold anymore!

There are bronzes and chocolates and blues and calicos and solids and blacks and whites and patches and many other combinations of the above. In addition to the wide scope of color variations comes numerous bodily aberrations as well. Upon reading further, you'll come to know the Lionhead, or Ranchu, the Ryukin, the Pearlscale, my personal favorite, the Bubble-Eye and others. While there are scores of various tropical fish to keep, I find none more charming and endearing than the goldfish.

The purpose of this book is not to turn you into a goldfish expert. The Chinese and Japanese have spent centuries doing this. Obviously, your interest has blossomed beyond a passing fancy, hence your purchase of this book. At this juncture, I expect you are at the point of discarding the bowl, basin, or even the bronze gelatin mold, and head into keeping some of the fancier varieties of goldfish. We are going to set our sights on how to successfully and properly care for your new family members.

Just as with any household pet, your goldfish have specific needs and requirements in order to maintain their well-being and liveliness. No, they are not particularly demanding, but they are living creatures. With a little care and minimal commitment you are sure to derive years of enjoyment and pride in keeping these neat little animals. After reading this book you should have no problem doing so. In fact, I think you'll find yourself even more enthusiastic.

This is an award-winning red Ryukin.

NATURAL HISTORY

All of the varieties of goldfish we see today are a result of mutation after mutation of wild carp originating from areas of eastern Asia. It is generally agreed that it was the Chinese who first began successfully breeding these fish. As they started to notice marked differences in the domestic offspring, they took steps to fix these strains. This practice has been traced back to over one thousand years ago. Subsequently, the Chinese passed on the acquired breeding techniques to the Japanese in the 1500s, and since then goldfish and their cousins, the koi, have been a mainstay to Japan. They have remained as popular today as they were almost five hundred years ago. The difference, however, is at one time fishkeeping was reserved for the noblemen, while we know today fishkeeping is for almost everyone.

It wasn't until the late 1800s that the goldfish made its way to the United States. It would have made a nice piece of folklore had the pilgrims marched off the Mayflower with a goldfish bowl in hand, but unfortunately for those of us who like to tell fish stories, it just didn't

This is a wild crucian carp from which goldfish are said to have derived.

happen that way. Actually, it was Rear Admiral Daniel Ammen who brought them back in 1878 to display in Washington, DC. They were a hit, and with regard to their popularity, let us say...the rest is "fishtory."

THE FAMILY ALBUM

Goldfish belong to a large family of fish known as the family Cyprinidae. This family includes other types of fish you may be familiar with such as koi, barbs, danios, rasboras and American minnows. Many aquarium cyprinids are warmwater species, but goldfish and koi are essentially coldwater fishes.

You will often see in aquarium literature Latin names being used to describe various species of fish. The scientific community, in an effort to reduce confusion derived from the use of "common" names, uses a system of naming all flora and fauna (plants and animals). This system gives a specific "scientific" name to a particular species to distinguish it from all the others. The scientific name of the goldfish is *Carassius auratus.*

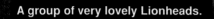

A group of very lovely Lionheads.

KEEPING GOLDFISH

"The goldfish is your perfect pet. You don't hafta walk it. It don't smell, it don't bark, and before you get too tired of it...it dies."-Archie Bunker

Now, to a certain extent most would-be goldfish keepers have found Archie Bunker's philosophy blunt, yet true. Our children bring home a goldfish from the school fair; we throw it in one sort of vessel or another, and add some additional tap water. In three days we find ourselves in the pet store trying to find an exact replica of Goldy before our kids come home from school to truly learn of their pet's fate. Accordingly, this little escapade could go on *ad infinitum*. While this certainly can be an opportunistic time to teach our young ones about death and dying, it doesn't necessarily have to be. The main thrust of this book is to give you advice on the proper care of goldfish be they a run-of-the-mill pool Comet or a lavish Calico Oranda.

The utmost is the Calico Oranda. This one has a growth like a crater!

PHOTO BY FRED ROSENZWEIG.

PHOTO BY FRED ROSENZWEIG.

A two pound male Calico Ryukin goldfish.

THE EQUIPMENT

"Buy the biggest tank you can afford." If you've been reading or talking to pet store professionals, you may have heard this quote several times. No, it is not a conspiracy between tank manufacturers and pet stores to raid your wallet. It is an effort to put you on the right track to successful fishkeeping from the beginning. It is natural to think, "I'll start small, and if I'm successful I'll move to a larger tank with better equipment then." Unfortunately, with living animals, if they're not treated properly from the start, they are ultimately doomed. Just what is the *right* equipment?

Let's start with the tank. Many people start with a bowl, but we really want to get away from that. To keep your fish healthy, a tank with sufficient surface area is a must. A fish bowl is like a toilet. The fish swims in it, goes to the bathroom in it, but who flushes it? You may add some water to compensate for evaporation, but the waste products just keep building up. Ammonia is a by-product of fish waste. This, combined with overfeeding (we'll hit on that later), leads your fish's bowl to become a veritable toxic waste dump. Even if you change the water on a regular basis, there is usually not sufficient volume to render the change effective.

What is a goldfish tank without some beautiful ornaments. There are many different SAFE ornaments for goldfish. Ask your local pet shop operator to show you some. Photo courtesy of Blue Ribbon who have the largest selection of goldfish ornaments.

Additionally, netting out the fish to perform this function causes stress to the fish and inevitable breakdown. With warmwater tropical fish, the general rule of thumb is one inch of fish per gallon of water. For example, that would equal 10-one inch fish to a 10-gallon tank. However, with goldfish this credo diminishes to half an inch of fish per gallon. In other words, that would equal 5 one-inch goldfish in ten gallons of water. Goldfish put out more bodily waste per gram of body weight than many warmwater tropical fish. The size is generally determined by measuring the fish from nose to base of tail. It won't be necessary to follow the fish around with a ruler; you can estimate with your eye.

Remember, if you are buying young fish their size will at least double in 6 months to a year. Some will triple, some will even quadruple in that time. When considering tank size, it is incumbent upon you to keep that fact in mind.

If you purchase a 10-gallon tank and place the maximum number of fish in it from the start as per the rule (5 inches) and they double in one year's time, you see how your tank has become overcrowded before you know it. A little forethought will tell you to purchase a 20-gallon tank for the same amount of fish, and in a year's time it will still be perfect. A 30-gallon tank will give you additional room to add several more fish over that period of time.

One final thought on choosing your tank. The lower, longer tanks are better for goldfish than the higher narrower ones. Goldfish require higher levels of oxygen than many other fish, and since oxygen saturation takes place at the surface level of the aquarium, the larger the surface area, the more oxygen penetrates the water surface.

FILTRATION

So many times I've heard statements like this. "I don't see why I need this filter...when I was a kid we kept fish in a bowl for 10 years, and we never had a problem." What is really meant is that they don't *remember* any problems. For however many reasons you can give me against filtration, I'll give you that many more for it.

There are a number of filtration systems on the market today. Some are expensive, some are not. For the purposes of this book, I will address two types of basic filtration systems and the purposes they serve: biological and mechanical. Each serves its own specific function as well as the function of the other. Any way you choose to employ them, both serve to improve water quality and help to keep it safe and healthy for your goldfish.

Mechanical Filtration

Generally speaking, mechanical filtration serves to filter out waste products as well as excessive debris from the water by passing the water through various media (carbon and foam) and returning it, cleaned, back to the aquarium. Mechanical filters are commonly known as the type that hang on the back of the tank with an

Keeping your aquarium clean, both inside (when it is emptied) and outside (when it can be full), requires a strong but safe cleaner. Your pet shop should have such a cleaner for your goldfish tank. Do not use sprays suitable for your home windows (glass cleaners!). They can kill fish.

intake tube that sits within the aquarium drawing the water into and through the filtration media. There are also completely submergible mechanical filters on the market today. The main function of mechanical filters is to keep the water clean, though they provide a certain amount of biological filtration as well.

Biological Filtration

Biological filtration is most commonly seen in the action of the undergravel filter. This is simply a plastic grooved plate that rests on the bottom of the tank and is subsequently covered with a sufficient gravel bed (1/2 to 2 inches). A partial vacuum is achieved by means of an air pump or water-pumping "power head," causing water to be pulled through the gravel, thus oxygenating the gravel bed. This process creates a medium in which beneficial bacteria grow. These bacteria break down fish waste into substances that are less harmful to the fish. This process is part of what is known as the nitrogen cycle.

It is highly recommended that both mechanical and biological filtration devices be used, as this will give you the optimum filtration for your aquarium. Using both methods of filtering along with other routine maintenance can increase your aquarium's capacity substantially. If you cannot afford both filters at the outset, it is simpler to install the undergravel unit first. You can always add the mechanical filter at a later date.

A very rare white Pearlscale goldfish.

PHOTO BY FRED ROSENZWEIG.

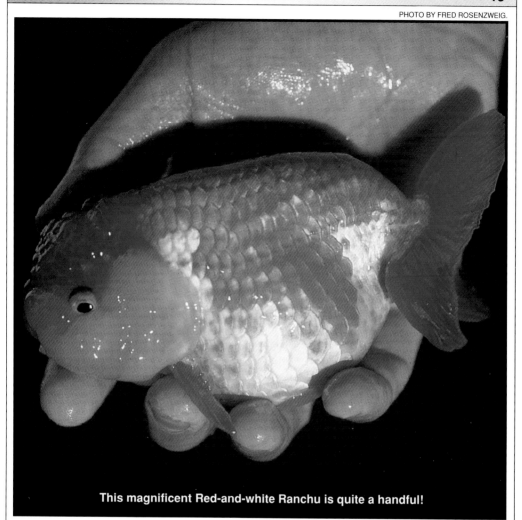
PHOTO BY FRED ROSENZWEIG.

This magnificent Red-and-white Ranchu is quite a handful!

ADDITIONAL EQUIPMENT

I always recommend a lighted fluorescent hood for the aquarium. Remembering that goldfish are coldwater fish, using incandescent bulbs that throw off a surprising amount of heat is not very conducive to your goldfish's well-being. The hood part of the fixture serves to reduce evaporation as well as keeping the fish *in* the tank. Yes, many a goldfish has been known to take a suicide leap out of the tank. From firsthand experience I can tell you that a dried goldfish is neither a pleasant sight nor a palatable gourmet item.

While goldfish do quite well in room temperature, it is also a good practice to keep a thermometer in the tank. This enables you to keep tabs on the water temperature in instances where extremes are a possibility.

Lastly, keep these two very important test kits on hand: pH and ammonia. These test kits are inexpensive and come in very handy during tank set-up periods as well as times when you may have to make preliminary diagnosis of your fish's health.

WATER QUALITY

Water from the tap may be good for you and me, but it could spell disaster for your fish. Unless your water comes from a ground well, the water supply that services your community more than likely has certain compounds not so desirable to fish life. These compounds, namely chlorine and chloramine as well as others to a lesser extent, are added to the water supply to prevent the buildup of harmful bacteria.

These substances are extremely irritating to the fish's gill membranes, and if they don't kill them, they could very well cause irreparable damage leading to an untimely death. You can buy products designed to neutralize the major gases added to water supplies, so you can treat a quantity and keep some in reserve. If you let the water sit for 24 hours or so, chlorine (but not chloramine) will dissipate on its own. And if you use an aerator to make the water

You simply must have a water test kit to enable you to maintain your goldfish pond, bowl or tank. A typical good kit measures pH, chlorine, ammonia, etc. Ask your pet shop to supply one AND BE SURE YOU USE IT ON A REGULAR WEEKLY BASIS! Photo courtesy of Aquarium Pharmaceuticals.

bubble vigorously, you'll dissipate it even faster. Your dealer can advise you about the best ways to "age" your water. The main thing to remember is that you shouldn't plunge your goldfish into raw tapwater.

Ammonia

As stated earlier in the filtration section, ammonia is a by-product of fish waste. There are several factors than can cause an increase of ammonia in the tank. Normally, a build-up of ammonia occurs in a system where the beneficial bacteria have not had a sufficient time to build themselves up and colonize. When this is the case, combined with an overload of fish wastes, a spike in the ammonia level will occur.

New systems generally require approximately 30 days to have the bacteria build up sufficiently to break down the ammonia. Ironically, this process can not begin until fish are added to the aquarium. Obviously, this puts your fish in a precarious position,

A Red-and-white Ranchu goldfish.

in that they are then subject to their own waste products which are essential in establishing the bacterial colony in the first place. What to do? Make your initial additions to the tank the inexpensive feeder fish.

Should you discover a sudden rise in your ammonia level after your initial set-up period, an immediate 1/3 water change should be made. A combination of high ammonia and a possible high pH is often fatal. After the water change there are commercially available resins you can add to your filter to remove any further ammonia. Take note, however, as to what caused this.

Did you add too many fish at one time?

Did you, or someone else, overfeed? Is there decay (fish or food) occurring in the tank?

How long has it been since your last water change?

It may not be a bad idea to add one of the commercially available ammonia detoxifying agents.

Use your ammonia test kit to monitor the ammonia's progress during this time. You want to see the level go way up, then drop to a zero reading. This is indicative of your tank's now being ready to accept fish safely.

pH

Very simply stated, pH is a measure of the water's acidity or alkalinity level. A 7.0 reading indicates a neutral state in the water, neither acid nor alkaline.

Normally, goldfish are easily acclimated to varying degrees of pH. If your tap water is far off the neutral scale to either side, it may be advantageous to use one of the pH modifiers on the market prior to introducing fish to the tank. Once situated, the fish might become accustomed to the water they are in, and future pH modification may not be necessary. Note that should you try your hand at breeding goldfish, the pH becomes a more important factor.

It is a good idea to know what the pH is of the water coming from your tap. Goldfish do fine in a slightly acid pH range of 6.8 to a slightly alkaline range of 7.4. Of course, extremes should be avoided. Common signs of adverse pH conditions include listlessness, gasping for air at the surface, reddening of the fins and gills, drooping fins, and lack of appetite.

New Tank Syndrome

This is simply a period of time soon after the tank has been set up during which the water turns cloudy.

Bubble-eyed Pom-pon brown Oranda. Goldfish don't get much fancier than this one!

PHOTO BY FRED ROSENZWEIG.

PHOTO BY FRED ROSENZWEIG.

A young, orange Lionhead.

What you will see happen as bacteria begin to colonize is that the tank water will turn a smoky white color. The smokiness will eventually disappear unless an unsanitary condition such as chronic overfeeding prevails. Basically, the tank is trying to achieve a certain equilibrium between the output of fish wastes and the number of bacteria necessary to break them down. In a sense the bacteria will build up enough to handle the level of waste output available. They can adjust accordingly, but there is time involved in this process. Be careful not to overload your aquarium during this period.

Salt in the Aquarium

Salt you say? Who puts salt in fresh water? Actually, if you think about it most freshwater systems do, in fact, have varying degrees of natural salts in them. It's not nearly as concentrated as natural seawater, but it is there just the same.

While goldfish, as well as other aquarium fish, can survive without salt added to the aquarium, the addition of one tablespoon per five gallons does wonders. Salt added to the water aids the fish with a biological process known as osmoregulation. Simply put, it is the process whereby oxygen is passed through the gill membranes. The easier this process is accomplished, the healthier the fish remains.

Salt added to the aquarium is better than any other disease preventative or remedy. These diseases generally afflict fish that are subject to stress. Ease in osmoregulation deters stress: less stress equals less chance of disease outbreak.

Water Evaporates, Salt Does Not

There will be times when you find it necessary to *top off* your aquarium water due to evaporation. When doing this, do not add any additional salt. However, when performing partial water changes, add only that much salt to compensate for the amount of water removed. If you remove 5 gallons of water, add 1 tablespoon of salt.

Do not use standard table salt. The aquarium salts on the market replicate more closely the naturally dissolved salts found in nature. Table salts usually contain non-binding agents to keep the salt from caking due to moisture. These caking agents can be dangerous to your fish's health.

Water Changes

The first 60 days of aquarium keeping are going to bring you to your first stage of routine tank maintenance...the partial water change.

A lovely, delicate Chinese Lionhead.

PHOTO BY FRED ROSENZWEIG.

Red-and-white Matt Ryukin.

Your filtration system will help to keep your water healthful for the fish, but it can't do the entire job. The biological filter will break down ammonia from fish waste into a less toxic substance known as nitrite. It will subsequently turn over the nitrite into an even less toxic substance known as nitrate. But partial water changes are still a good idea.

It is recommended that a goldfish tank have part of its water changed regularly. Every two weeks you should remove a third of the water and replace it with aged dechlorinated fresh water. If you perform this function regularly, the chance of your fish contracting disease will be minimized significantly.

You can use a regular aquarium siphon that will help you to clean your gravel bed at the same time. What you want to

A new variety of goldfish called Panda Telescope-eyed goldfish.

do is start the siphon going per the directions. Push the siphon into the gravel bed. You see the siphon pick up gravel and swirl it around. Pull the siphon out of the gravel, leaving it in the water, you will see the gravel fall down, while any accumulated debris will go up and out. Repeat this process in different spots of the gravel until the appropriate amount of water has been removed.

Another option, especially if you have a very large tank or multiple tanks, is the automatic water changers that attach directly to your water source. They work by way of water pressure. In one position the water will drain, while in the opposite position the tank will fill. Remember when filling to be wary of filling with too much tap water that contains chlorine. One option is to refill part way with the tap water, and fill the remainder with aged water you have stored.

A youthful high-humped Red Ryukin.

PHOTO BY FRED ROSENZWEIG.

FEEDING

To this day, I still remember the children's book about the goldfish that was overfed. Remember the little boy was told by the kindly old pet store owner to only feed him a little bit twice a day? The little boy took his goldfish home, and after feeding the prescribed amount noticed how sad and hungry his little goldfish looked. So he fed him a little more. The goldfish still looked hungry, so he fed him a little more. The more the boy fed him, the hungrier he looked, and the more he grew. He was eventually busting out of his fish bowl. The goldfish grew larger than a shark, and this poor little boy had a disaster on his hands...all because he didn't listen to the pet store owner.

The moral of this story: Goldfish *always* look hungry, don't believe what you see.

While most goldfish don't require a special diet, they do require a varied diet. Unfortunately for the goldfish, most goldfish owners buy one can of flake food, and keep feeding them that same food day after day, month after month, year after year. Most of these commercially available foods satisfy basic dietary requirements, but they don't satisfy them all.

Diet

I feed my goldfish twice a day, morning and evening. For convenience purposes (usually morning) I feed one of the flake foods. However, I do vary the flakes that I use. The purpose of varying the flakes is simply to provide a greater variety of nutrients, since different brands of flake foods contain different mixes of ingredients. All in all, what you're doing is varying the diet while benefiting from the ease of feeding a flaked food.

Goldfish thrive on greens. Usually, it is the evening where I choose to get a little more gourmet with the fish's diet. Goldfish will feast on a variety of greens. The easiest way to prepare these foods is par-boiling (half-boiling). You can cut slices of zucchini, par-boil them, put them in a plastic freezer bag, and feed them at will. Peas are also a favorite, along with spinach, watercress, endive, and various assorted green vegetables. Don't feed them iceberg lettuce. It has   little nutritional value, and is

PHOTO COURTESY OF WARDLEY.

Flake foods are eagerly taken by goldfish. Only feed quality flake foods made especially for goldfish. Tropical fish flake foods are not satisfactory for coldwater fish like goldfish.

A group of magnificent Calico Orandas.

therefore a waste of food and time.

If you really want to provide your pets with a treat, you can try some of the frozen foods available such as bloodworms, brine shrimp, prawn, daphnia, or even some of the foods designed for saltwater fish. It's an even better treat if you can provide the real living thing to them on occasion.

How much?

One of the worst things for a goldfish's health is overfeeding. Most of us have a tendency to overfeed our fish as we sometimes overfeed ourselves. Nature has a funny way of doing everything perfect. Every now and then we need to take a lesson from Mother Nature. Why do fish always look hungry? Because they normally should be. In their natural habitat, fish are constantly scavenging for food. Feeding is an opportunistic event, and fish in their natural environment have the natural instincts to eat what's available, when it's available. There is normally never enough to keep their appetites completely satiated.

Conversely, in our aquariums, if we feed too much the fish will take advantage of this opportunity and eat everything we give them. Nature tells them to look for more. This can lead to adverse health conditions as well as adverse water conditions if this practice continues. It is always better to err on the side of underfeeding. The fish will thrive when they have to forage rather than feast.

It is also a good practice to fast your fish once a week. This forces the fish to forage the bottom of the tank for any possible leftovers. If they've been overfed, it gives them a chance to clean out their systems, and keeps the tank free of uneaten food at the same time.

Red-and-white (often referred to in the goldfish trade as *white-and-red*)Veiltail Ryukin goldfish.

PHOTO BY FRED ROSENZWEIG.

GOLDFISH DISEASES

You've read everything so far on how to keep your fish healthy, and you've followed all of my advice to the letter. You purchase healthy vibrant looking stock from a reputable dealer, and now some, or all, of your fish are sick. Where did you go wrong?

It is not the intention of this book to turn you into a fish pathologist, just as it not the intention to instantly turn you into a goldfish expert. There are far more comprehensive texts on both subjects. What I want to do is make you realize what you should look for, what caused it, and what you can do about it.

If you are a parent, you know you don't need to be a doctor to know that your child is ill. You can just tell. You have developed a sixth sense about it. You get a feeling, just by looking. In time you will develop this same ability when it comes to your fish. Until then, I'll give you some things you can look for.

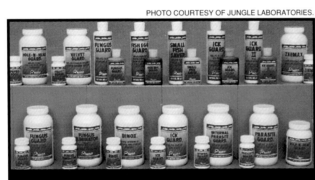

PHOTO COURTESY OF JUNGLE LABORATORIES.

Many different remedies, preventatives and tonics are available at pet shops.

Ichthyophthirius

What? We call it *ich* for short. This is a tiny parasite that spreads itself all over the fish and shows up like someone mistook your fish for french fries, pouring salt all over them.

Ich can be brought on or brought in. There are always ever-present organisms brewing within your aquarium. A fish's normal immune system generally wards them off, but if the fish is subject to stress (poor water quality, poor nutrition, over aggressiveness by a tankmate) the immune system can and will break down. This leaves the fish susceptible to a range of diseases.

You should suspend feeding and raise the tank temperature gradually (over a period of 48 hours) to around 85 degrees Fahrenheit. This speeds up the life cycle of the cyst, thus eradicating it. Gradually lower the temperature when the spots are no longer visible and resume your feeding schedule. It wouldn't hurt to give them a

Goldfish can be pets and can be hand fed! You can tame and train your goldfish.

GOLDFISH DISEASES

daily dose of the aloe formula on the market. This also aids in the healing process for any wounds left over from the ich infestation.

Remembering that goldfish are coldwater fish, this high temperature may add to the fish's stress level. It is essential that your tank contains the salt as earlier prescribed. You must also keep a very close eye on them during this two day period. At times they may gasp for air at the tank surface. Hopefully upon resumption of their normal tank temperature, their resiliency will return.

The other way of contracting ich is bringing it in. When selecting your goldfish look for signs of trouble. If you think something's wrong, trust your instinct. Something probably is, so don't buy it. A healthy goldfish will have clear eyes, swim strongly, and carry its fins erect. If the fish looks droopy or listless, or has blemishes on its skin...avoid it. Also, avoid any other fish available in the same tank. Additionally, be wary of any store that is willing to sell you fish that are obviously diseased.

Quarantine Tank

When I talk to people about keeping a separate tank for housing their fish prior to introducing them into their pre-existing community tank, I am usually met with hesitance and skepticism.

A sure sign of serious trouble is when the goldfish come to the surface and gasp for air. Immediate rescue can be achieved by spraying the top of the pond with a garden hose or using a very turbulent air pump to agitate the water. This rids the water of excess carbon dioxide and allows the fish to utilize the oxygen.

This red Comet goldfish has been attacked by anchor worms which have caused an infection at their site of attachment.

Most of you reading this are having your first experience with fish. You are having enough trouble getting one tank started, let alone thinking about buying a separate one. It's not a bad idea, though. Let me explain further. All a quarantine tank has to be is a small undecorated tank with a very inexpensive corner filter. You can keep it in an out-of-the-way place. When you purchase a new fish, he goes into this tank for two weeks or so, until it is determined they are not sick, nor will they transmit any disease to your healthy fish community. Most beginners do not go this route, and you don't have to. However, be careful. One diseased fish can wipe out your whole stock.

YOU'VE HEARD IT BEFORE: AN OUNCE OF PREVENTION IS WORTH A POUND OF CURE!

Anchor Worms

Yecch! This is a visible parasite that more than likely came in with your purchase. You must physically remove them. Its name is derived from its shape; that of a ship's anchor.

Remove the fish from the tank, holding it within a wet washcloth. Using a blunt pinching device (tweezers, hemostats, etc.), grip the worm as close as possible at the point of attachment, and give a swift, but steady pull. To avoid any possible infection, dab the wounded area with mercurochrome. Perform this operation as quickly as possible for obvious reasons. It wouldn't be a bad idea to have assistance as well.

You will want to check with a pet store professional for a suitable treatment for any remaining free swimming worms still in the juvenile stage. Don't forget to check the rest of fish as well!

Dropsy

If you took your fish, filled him up with air to the point just prior to explosion, this would be indicative of a fish maligned with dropsy. Another name for this affliction is *pinecone disease* inasmuch as the raised scales give the fish the appearance of a pinecone.

The cause of dropsy is believed to be bacterial or viral, though poor water quality is the culprit more likely than not. It would be advisable to remove the fish to a separate tank (here's that quarantine suggestion again!) making sure the water quality there is optimal. It also goes without saying to check all of the water conditions in your display tank. Additionally, check your other fishes to ascertain whether any others are showing any of the same symptoms.

Other signs

Other fish ailments most often brought about by poor water quality include fin rot, fungus and velvet.

Other parasites seen, usually brought in by the fish, include fish lice, gill flukes and skin flukes. If you suspect parasites, seek the advice of an aquarium professional.

Floating Disease

Here's a scenario: You come home one evening, and to your dismay you find your favorite Oranda or Ryukin floating at the top of the tank. You hasten over to check on him as this is not his usual behavior, and find yourself relieved at the fact that he is, in fact, alive.

All of the other aquarium members are swimming joyfully around the tank, while this guy just hangs around the surface of the water. When feeding time approaches he struggles almost aimlessly to gulp at the food, eventually making his way back

This goldfish is suffering from dropsy. Its body is bloated (more so than normal) and its scales are protruding.

This Calico Shubunkin is in distress. Its fins are clamped and it lays listlessly on the bottom of the tank. It should be removed to a nursery (=quarantine) tank and medicated.

to the upper corner of the tank. Every day he seems more and more listless. There are no outward signs of disease. You've checked your water quality and everything seems normal. What could be wrong?

Two days later, upon arriving home you see a shadow out of the corner of your eye floating upside down. Upon inspection you are shocked to see that he is *still* alive. Upside down, but alive. What is going on here?

More than likely it is what is referred to as swim bladder disease. I've already described the symptom of the disease, but what is a swim bladder, and what can be done to cure this disease?

A swim bladder is an internal organ in most fish that allow them to remain buoyant. The amount of gas in the bladder is regulated by the fish depending on it's desire to stay at the top of the water column, hover in the middle, or sink to the bottom. You've probably heard the fact that sharks must remain in constant motion in order to survive. This is due, in part, to the fact that they have no swim bladder. They must stay in constant motion to force oxygen through their gills or they will sink to the bottom and die.

Fancy goldfish are more susceptible than the common Comet goldfish and are more susceptible due to their genetically altered body shapes. There are several factors that can bring about swim bladder disorder. These factors include: sudden temperature drop, bacterial infections and genetic disorders. Primarily, however, the cause is all too often *incorrect feeding.*

As stated in the feeding section, many goldfish owners keep their fish on a staple diet of fish flakes.

Many times the flakes purchased are the cheapest ones on the market. After all, that's what you always fed your fish when you were a kid, and he did great...or did he? A constant and continuous diet such as this often leads to constipation.

Blocked intestines can and will interfere with the function of the swim bladder. If this is the case, a cure is easy to effect. First things first, check your water. If you are not using salt, gradually add it to the tank over a twelve hour period. Fast the fish for four days. Don't worry! A hungry fish is better than a dead one. This will enable the fish to clear itself out, and normal function of the swim bladder should return. After the fourth day, resume feeding with live or frozen brine shrimp. By this time you should have learned your lesson, and will go on to provide your goldfish with a more nutritious well-balanced diet as recommended earlier.

If after this period the fish has gotten no better, the disease is more than likely congenital. Unfortunately there is no cure for this fish and it should be destroyed. As many of us do get attached to our wet friends it is hard to just net him out and flush him down the toilet. One very safe and humane way of killing a fish is freezing.

Scoop out the poor guy and wrap him in a wet paper towel. Place the wrapped body in a plastic freezer bag, laying him in the freezer. As the fish freezes, his metabolism will gradually slow down, placing him into a comatose state prior to final expiration. If there are young children involved, once the fish is frozen, you can have a burial ceremony. This may sound a bit silly to some, but this is actually a good way to expose young ones to death.

I was personally shocked when I found out my eight-year-old son had performed his own funeral for a Redcap Oranda, complete with burial marker. I almost stepped on it while mowing the lawn. I felt badly that I hadn't shown more compassion when the fish died. I could have been more of a comfort to him.

This Shubunkin is having trouble excreting and has a blocked intestinal tract. Read this chapter to learn how to treat this common disorder.

PHOTO BY MARY E. SWEENEY.

If you really want to do it right, follow the layout of this outdoor pond.

PONDKEEPING

Quite often, pondkeeping and goldfish keeping are subjects featuring a number of parallels. There are goldfish that can be kept in outdoor ponds, as well as outdoor pondfish that do quite well in indoor aquaria.

Pondkeeping has risen to an art form arguably, perfected by the Japanese, and respectfully imitated by the rest of the world. Many people keeping goldfish find themselves intrigued by these pets and are subsequently drawn outdoors by the opportunity of providing their fish with a more natural, environmentally friendly home.

THE POND

Ponds can be built or installed in a wide variety of shapes, sizes and designs. You can purchase a *pre-formed* pond, or excavate the pond yourself using a poly-butyl vinyl liner.

The preforms and/or liners are available at most pet stores or garden supply centers. The pond liners are sold in various sizes and can be shaped to your desire.

Digging a pond is quite a physical undertaking, and a sufficient amount of planning should be involved prior to digging the first shovelful. Factors needed to be taken into consideration include drainage, shading, protection from natural wildlife, and filtration options.

The pond should be situated in a sloped area or built to accommodate overflow to prevent flooding. The pond should not be situated in direct sunlight. In addition to the possibility of overheating the pond, especially during the summer months, exposure to direct sunlight will lead to an

This is a typical goldfish/koi pond in Japan.

unsightly pool of green algae canvassing your sparkling fish pond. You want to make sure that your pond is not too accessible to fish-eating wildlife (raccoons, opossums, birds, etc.). If you reside in an area that is often visited by these creatures, you will need to take the proper precautions to protect your fish. If you desire to employ mechanical/biological filtration devices you will have to have the pond situated in an area accessible to electrical power or have electrical service installed close to the pond.

I am barely scraping the surface of information associated with pondkeeping. If you are even remotely interested in pursuing this quest, I strongly recommend that you seek further information on this topic. TFH Publications offers several volumes on pondkeeping well authored and illustrated.

Pondkeeping can be an extremely rewarding hobby, as well as a pleasant addition to your home's landscape. There is significant expense and

PHOTO BY DR. HERBERT R. AXELROD.

labor involved. My eight-year-old son has been begging me for a pond. My answer to him is, "When you can dig it, you can have it!"

Follow up your interest with research. It will only enhance your pursuit.

Pondfish

There are several types of fish that make good pond inhabitants. The most popular pond-kept fish, however are goldfish and *nishikigoi,* or as they are more popularly known in English speaking countries, *koi.*

Right: A grand champion Kohaku koi over 30 inches long and owned by Takeshi Hayashi.

Below: This is a lovely English-style goldfish/koi pond.

Coldwater fish, goldfish and koi (*Cyprinus carpio*) do well in most outdoor environments, barring severe extremes, of course. Some keepers residing in the colder winter climates opt to bring their fish indoors for the winter. There are people who actually construct pond set-ups inside their homes to house their fish during the off-season.

Providing your outdoor pond will not freeze solid, you can keep them in the pond year 'round. Feedings, however should be limited during the winter as the fish's metabolism slows down significantly, and any uneaten food can pollute the water.

A grand champion Showa Sanshoku koi about 29 inches owned by the Ikenaga Nishikigoi Center in Japan.

An American two-level pond with running water. A pump takes the water from the base of the pond and pumps it, via hidden water lines, to the top of the pond thus utilizing the drop in elevation to make a natural waterfall.

A do-it-yourself waterfall used for decoration and aeration of a koi and goldfish pond.

Goldfish in the Pond

While all goldfish are coldwater fish, not all goldfish do well in a pond environment. The stout heavy-bodied fancy varieties often have trouble surviving in outdoor pond conditions. They especially have trouble if they are forced to compete for food with their sleek torpedo-shaped cousins, namely Comets, Shubunkins and koi.

Comets are basically the cute little goldfish we're all too familiar with. While they can grow almost as large as their relatives, the koi, they differ in their dorsal fin base as well as having a forked tail. Don't worry, a forked tail is not the same as a forked tongue, Kimosabe! They do make excellent pondmates, though.

Shubunkins are the scaleless variety in the goldfish family. They are cigar-shaped with a single forked tail. Their traits will be mentioned in a following chapter.

Koi represent a large topic indeed. The Japanese lust after a fine specimen of koi sometimes paying in the tens of thousands of dollars for one single creature. Just as with goldfish, there are numerous varieties of koi differing in color, shape, scale placement, and tail configuration. Basically, koi are common carp. Through inbreeding, colors, color patterns, and fin shape, all more desirous than that of their native brothers, has been developed.

Add to their beauty the fact that koi are extremely resilient and can often survive the foulest of conditions, this makes them excellent pond inhabitants. This, of course, is not to say they should be neglected. Rather, suffice it to say they can withstand the hazards placed upon them by both man and nature.

The pond-side pagoda and lovely statuary makes this a goldfish pond with an Oriental flavor.

PHOTO BY MARY E. SWEENEY

There is hardly any decoration for a home that is more interesting or more beautiful than a goldfish pond.

Now, combine their beauty with their resiliency, and add to that mixture a hint of charm and you have what one might refer to as a pet. Koi will recognize their specific caretaker (feeder). They will clamor to the surface the moment your arrival is noticed with mouths-a-gapin' and tails-a-waggin'. While this is more than likely a condition-response mechanism (you feed, we come) the fish almost certainly recognizes you as the primary feeder, and may or may not react the same to a stranger approaching.

It is this recognition factor that endears them to their keepers. Talk to any koi keeper and you will be amazed at how attached someone can become to a fish.

Today you can find simple pond set-ups in backyards of many homes. San Francisco's Golden Gate Park features an entire area designed to replicate the ponds of Japan, known as The Japanese Tea Gardens. Some sport single or multiple waterfalls, some have elaborately fashioned fountains, while others are so large that bridges to span them must be included in the design. Not only are ponds gaining more and more popularity in the home, but they are also being included in the architecture of office buildings, hotels, and shopping malls, just to name a few. There are countless more variations to this theme than can be accounted for in this volume.

Wherever the degree of your interest in pondkeeping may lie, you are sure to derive great amounts of pleasure and pride from your endeavor. Be sure to research as much as possible with all of the available literature you can as well as the experiences of others.

A Red-cap Oranda is not really a pond fish because it is a weak swimmer. Red-cap Orandas are best kept in tanks.

PHOTO BY FRED ROSENZWEIG.

PHOTO BY MARY E. SWEENEY.

This could have been a wonderful pond but the algae have taken over and the pond is pea-soup green. The major problem with goldfish ponds is that they are subject to often fatal algal attacks. You must have sufficient plant cover (water lilies and floating plants) so that the algae can't survive.

VARIETIES OF GOLDFISH

As pointed out in the beginning of this book, goldfish are not limited to those plain little dart-shaped fish you used to see all the time as a youngster at school fairs, carnivals and 5 & 10's. There are a number of varieties, not only in size, but shape, color, eye types, fin types, scale types and others as well. While most of these forms can be kept together in a community, remember that all goldfish are very opportunistic feeders. That is, the more they can individually scarf up, the more they will.

Comets and Shubunkins grab food more hastily than the other deeper-bodied Orandas and Ryukins. Orandas and Ryukins maneuver more adeptly than the slightly less adroit Lionheads and Pearlscales, while the Telescope-Eyes and Bubble-Eyes are the most awkward

The Comet goldfish is the most popular of all goldfish because it is the least expensive and is available in most pet shops.

foragers of all.

While all varieties can very well exist with one another, you have to be very keen to make sure everyone is getting the necessary amount of food. Lastly, don't forget to follow the feeding requirements as outlined in this book. You will learn to love these unusual, yet fascinating creatures.

The Comet

This is by far the most common goldfish of the pack. As mentioned so many times, this is the goldfish you all too often see being given away at carnivals and such.

These fellows are also sold *en masse* as feeders for other carnivorous aquarium fish. They are bred by the millions in Florida fish farms primarily for this purpose, though I'm sure millions more become pets living on for years and years.

While many are seen in aquarium stores as small as one-half inch in length, they grow quickly and can reach a size of six to eight inches in a year's time. Over a period of several years, they can attain a size of 12 inches. At this size they often outgrow their indoor aquaria, though they would make excellent pond fish.

As they are often sold very young, many are still jacketed in their drab olive gray juvenile

A Red-and-white Ryukin goldfish.

coloration. As they grow their succeeding adult coloration intensifies. Comets are available in a number of colors and color combinations: Red, red and white, black, red and black, white and calico.

The Comet, with its single forked tail, is an extremely fast fish and aggressive feeder. Therefore, it is not advisable to keep larger Comets with the slower heavy bodied fancy goldfish. They will not be able to compete with the swift Comet for food.

Many people start off with Comets, and advance to keeping tropical fish, utilizing the same aquarium set up. While Comets, and other goldfish as well, are good peaceful tankmates, remember they are coldwater fish. When you add a heater to accommodate the tropicals, you create an environment not necessarily conducive to goldfish. Regardless, many have had their goldfish adapt nicely to the tropical aquarium. However, if you are looking to keep and raise high quality fancy goldfish (perhaps even breed them at a later date), this becomes more of a factor.

Ryukins

One of the most popular yet inexpensive of the fancy goldfish on the market today is the Ryukin. Also known as the Japanese Fantail, the Ryukin is a

PHOTOS BY FRED ROSENZWEIG.

A major award winning super white Ryukin.

An award winning high hump Red-and-white Ryukin.

PHOTOS BY FRED ROSENZWEIG.

very hearty variety of goldfish. Long flowing fins are characteristic of the breed and give it a majestic, yet playful appearance. Ryukins are also known as Veiltails. Aptly named is this fin type as its long flowing tail resembles a long billowy wedding veil.

Of all the fancy varieties, the Ryukin is the strongest swimmer and would be the most likely to fare well in a pond situation. This is not strongly recommended although the possibility does exist.

Ryukins can be found in red, red and white, red and black, and calico. Occasionally they are also seen in bronze.

A pair of young, award winning Ryukins.

A two pound Calico Ryukin.

Eye Types

There are three varieties of goldfish that sport unusual eye types. Both their fins and bodies are shorter than that of the Ryukin. These three types are the Telescope-Eye, the Celestial-Eye, and the Bubble-Eye.

A very rare White Pom-pon Fantail Telescope-eye goldfish.

The Telescope-Eye

The Telescope-Eye derives its name from the bulging tube shaped appendages emanating from its head into which its eyes are set. These extremities may protrude as much as one-half inch from the head.

There are three eye types that characterize the Telescope-Eye goldfish.

Spheroid Eye: This eye type resembles a bisected globe attached to the side of the head. Of the three shapes, this is the

Above: A young Panda Telescope-eye. Below: Orange-and-white Broadtail Telescope-eye.

PHOTOS BY FRED ROSENZWEIG.

Butterfly-tail Calico Telescope-eye.

A pair of Panda Telescope-eye goldfish.

largest. The base of the eye protuberance covers almost the entire side of the fish's head. An example of this eye would be represented by the Black Moor.

Oval Eye: The oval eye extends further from the head than the spheroid, but with a much smaller base.

Cone Shape: The cone shape eye has a large base and extends from the head tapering to a rounded point protruding from the head.

Standards state that the Telescope-Eye should be a short, ovular round-bodied fish. In adults the tail should be equal in length to the body. Eye sets should be symmetrical.

The Telescope-Eye has quite a number of variations: eye type,

This blue caste Telescope-eye is an extreme rarity.

PHOTO BY FRED ROSENZWEIG

color, and now add to that scale type. You can find Telescope Eyes with pearlescent (nacreous) scales, metallic scales, scales that have a flat finish (matt) and pearlscale.

There is also a rarely seen Telescope-Eye with a bubbly headgrowth known as a Dragonhead. The color varieties that you see Telescope-Eyes available in are red, red and white, calico, brown, Redcap, sometimes red & black and a solid black matt variety referred to as the Black Moor.

The Black Moor goldfish.

The Black Moor

The Black Moor is one of the most popular of the Telescope-Eye goldfish in the hobby today. It's eyes bulge out from it's head amidst a flat colored charcoal body. Very young Black Moors are olive in color and darken with age. Some begin to bronze at an even older age, though high quality specimens generally

A show-quality Black Moor goldfish.

PHOTO BY FRED ROSENZWEIG.

retain their deep black color for life.

There are two tail types associated with the Black Moor, the broadtail and the fantail. The broadtail has the same body type and finnage as the common Fantail, but with more flowing veil-like fins and no forking in the tailfin. The fantail is the more readily available variety with shorter fins in general.

Again, monitor water quality. Poor water can lead to the development of cataracts in Telescope-Eyes.

Celestial-Eyes

Unlike the Telescope-Eye, the Celestial-Eyes have a long tapered body and are conspicuous by the absence of a dorsal fin. They are named Celestial-Eyes as their

Head-on vision of Celestial goldfish.

A Celestial-eye goldfish.

large protruding spheroid eyes are positioned in such a way that they seem to be forever looking upward into the heavens. The upward looking pupil aids in accentuating this characteristic.

The upturned eye is not present at birth. This characteristic generally presents itself at approximately four months of age. As with many matters of Chinese origin, there lies an attached fable. One fable mentions that these fish were kept in covered jars, with only a slit in the cover. The fish subsequently turned their eyes upward to seek out the source of light.

A second story reads that these fish were purposely developed to honor a Chinese Emperor. He found it very appealing to have a fish that gazed upon him

A Celestial-eye goldfish.

whenever he chose to gaze upon them. How's that for satisfying one's ego!

There are two tail types connected with the Celestial-Eye. Those with *double tail* fins have medium length finnage with the tail fin measuring approximately three-fourths of the body length. Those with single *forked* tails should hold them high and erect above the body.

Celestial-Eyes can reach a length upwards of nine inches. Generally they are seen in color variations consisting of all red or a yellowish orange and white combination. They are, perhaps, the worst variety of goldfish when it comes to visual acuity. Remember to monitor their food intake carefully if you are keeping them with other varieties.

Bubble-Eyes

As I mentioned in the opening of this book, the Bubble-Eye is one of my favorites. There is something so genuinely endearing about this fish's countenance. Suspended under each eye is a fluid filled bubble, or sac.

Combining the bubbles with the upwardly turned eyes (similar to the Celestial-Eye) they present the

A variation of both the Celestial and the Bubble-eye is the Pearl Toad Head (Hama Tou). It is a weird and delicate fish.

PHOTO BY A. ROTH.

appearance of a little puppy who has just been scolded.

Not unlike the Celestial-Eye, the Bubble-Eye has a long torpedo-shaped body and no dorsal fin. The bubble sacs can vary in both size and thickness. A Chinese variety sports a shorter body with smaller, yet firmer bubbles. Usually, the larger the bubble, the thinner the skin. Larger bubbles are often weightier, forcing the fish to spend much of its time on the floor of the aquarium resting its bubbles on the gravel bed. Inasmuch as the fish does rest so often on the gravel, it is important that the gravel be a smooth, rounded variety in order to avoid

A red and an orange Celestial-eye.

PHOTO BY FRED ROSENZWEIG.

A Bubble-eye goldfish with eye sacs so heavy it can hardly move.

PHOTO BY FRED ROSENZWEIG.

This black Celestial-eye would be a champion if it didn't have the rudimentary growth where the dorsal fin used to be.

damaging or bursting the bubble. Burst bubbles can heal, but they are usually not as symmetrical and as large as the original ones.

Larger, longer aquariums are especially recommended for the Bubble-Eyes, essentially to diffuse the current put out by the power filters. It is best, though, to avoid power filters with very strong intake/output currents (many internal power filters) as this can prove to be quite uncomfortable for the Bubble-Eye. A smaller than usually recommended power filter set at the extreme end of the aquarium combined with a sponge filter is generally sufficient and safe.

Additional care must also be exercised whenever it is necessary to move the Bubble-Eye from its tank. Netting should be completely avoided. So too should be hand scooping. Both of these methods could cause damage to the fish's bubble sacs. Rather, they should be gently guided into a bag or bowl from inside of the aquarium.

Bubble-Eyes can reach a length of four to eight inches depending upon their body type. The shorter Chinese variety will usually be on the smaller end of the scale, while the longer bodied version will lean toward the larger end. If properly cared for, the bubble sacs will continue to grow throughout the fish's life. Bubble-Eyes are usually seen in color varieties of red, red and white, black, bronze, calico and blue scale.

A Bubble-eye goldfish.

PHOTO BY FRED ROSENZWEIG.

The Lionhead

Otherwise referred to as the Ranchu, the Lionhead is distinctly characterized by a bubbly headgrowth called a *wen*. This odd-looking growth, to a degree, resembles a lion's mane, hence the name.

The Lionhead is a short stocky fish with no dorsal fin. The Japanese refer to the Lionhead as the king of the goldfish, with the wen forming its crown. The wen will continue to grow throughout the life of the fish. During certain growth stages, white pustules appear about the head of the fish.

PHOTO BY FRED ROSENZWEIG.

A group of USA (American bred) Ranchus.

These are often mistaken by aquarists as forms of disease or fungus, and treated as such.

A phenomenal matt-scaled Bubble-eye.

PHOTO BY FRED ROSENZWEIG

A wonderful two-year old Ranchu.

These poor guys are forced to take medicine when nothing is wrong. These pustules are actually indicative of normal growth of the wen. These pustules form the bubbly wart-like appendages that make up the wen, similar to a rosebud waiting to bloom.

The Lionhead has a short broad tail and should be carried high, slightly above the back, and be evenly divided on both sides. While the Lionhead is not nearly as sedentary as the Bubble-Eye, it is one of the most awkward swimmers. As their bodies are so stocky, and their fins so comparatively short, they seem to waddle through the water. Watching them wiggle around is often a very humorous spectacle.

Be careful when purchasing Lionheads. Their backs should be smooth, rising from the head and sloping toward the tail. Very often

A Red-and-white Ranchu.

A huge red Oranda weighing over two pounds.

does not always have the best vision. This is often perpetuated by the wen growth reaching over the eyes. Take care to make sure your Lionhead is receiving the proper and adequate nutrition. It is strongly believed that a diet rich in greens will promote an even better headgrowth.

The Oranda

One of the largest, most varied breeds of goldfish is the Oranda. While the body of the Oranda is short, it is not as stout as the Ryukin or Lionhead. A good specimen will have nice sized fins similar to the Ryukin with a pronounced dorsal fin as well. It also has similarities to the Lionhead in that the Oranda also sports a wen (head growth),

you will find less than perfect specimens with a bony ridgy backbone. This could lead to health problems in the future.

As with so many of the fancy goldfish breeds, the Lionhead

This Oranda has an outstanding head growth.

A Calico Ryukin Oranda.

though not as prominent. With both of these similarities present in the breed, it is sometimes theorized that the Oranda is a cross between the Ryukin and the Lionhead.

This theory has been contradicted, however, by various experts in the field. The contentions are that, despite numerous breedings of the Oranda, there has never been any resulting progeny lacking the dorsal fin, a distinct characteristic of the Lionhead. Genetically speaking, if the Oranda did, in fact, have ancestry going back to the Lionhead, one would expect a certain number of Orandas to be lacking a dorsal fin. At this point,

let's leave any further hypothetical situations to the experts.

The head growth in Orandas develop at a later stage than the Lionheads. Keep in mind when purchasing either, young specimens offered for sale should have at least the beginnings of some headgrowth. Be wary of those being sold as Orandas with no head growth whatsoever.

Orandas can obtain a body length of ten to twelve inches, and a body weight sometimes exceeding two pounds. This makes for one impressive fish. Orandas, too, are offered in a wide variety of colors. Their colors include solid red, red and white,

PHOTO BY FRED ROSENZWEIG.

A pair of Redcap Orandas affectionately called *gooseheads* in the USA.

orange-yellow, blue, bronze (sometimes referred to as chocolate) and calico.

Additionally there are two other form variations of the Oranda.

Redcap Oranda

Essentially, a Redcap is an Oranda that is completely white, save for its wen which is completely red. This contrasting scheme makes for a strikingly brilliant fish. Within this variety you may find several variations in body size, fin length and the presence or absence of a dorsal fin.

A pair of Pom-pon Orandas.

PHOTO BY A. ROTH.

Pom-pon Orandas

The unusual feature displayed on this variety emanates from the nasal area of the fish. Often labeled as Pom-pon Orandas, this nomenclature is most likely derived from the "pom-pom"-like nasal projections. Frankly speaking, this fish looks as if it blew its nose and forgot to wipe.

These projections, more properly referred to as naris,

Redcap Oranda.

PHOTO BY FRED ROSENZWEIG

bobble about above the nose giving the fish a very clown-like appearance.

The Pom-pon is generally seen in color variations of red, red and white, and less often in some other standard goldfish coloration.

The Pearlscale

All goldfish varieties have identical scale shape and structure except for the Pearlscale. In normal scale structure the scale lays flat, one atop the other, similar to a shingled roof. In the Pearlscale the center of the scale projects